I keep it on my nightstand and refer to it when I need a little pick-me-up or a reminder to take action for my well-being.

Jessie G., RN

Bruce Schmidt provides us with a powerful and concise mental health guide. It offers practical advice that can be easily applied to everyday life, addressing common issues such as stress, anxiety, and situational depression. Readers will appreciate the humor and well-honed advice from this highly regarded, seasoned practitioner. Health care professionals will find this a crucial resource for patient education and awareness, enhancing their ability to provide comprehensive care. This book is a timely addition to the field!

Rebekah Radmanesh, MD
Board Certified Psychiatrist

This book is designed to make readers feel understood and less alone. It reassures us that life's ups and downs are more normal than we thought. It aims to demystify emotional challenges using everyday language. This book offers real-world tactics that speak to you in plain language.

Richard F., JD

My personal connection with Bruce spans more than 20 years, both as a friend and a valued colleague. We have collaborated on the care of hundreds of patients, and his insights have always been invaluable. This guide is a straightforward approach to dealing with life's obstacles, offering a personal touch that makes it feel like a conversation with a trusted friend. His insights will help you better understand yourself and your overall well-being. In addition, Bruce has included some of his favorite recipes (many of which I have had the pleasure to enjoy), which enhance the value of this guide and make it feel even more personal.

Shari D. Cohen, MD
Internist

A must-have resource for all who think they're the only ones feeling unsettled. In a time when mental health professionals are hard to access, it's nice to have a resource to begin your journey to better mental health and happiness. Bruce has managed many of my cancer patients and is an invaluable resource.

Maggi Coplin, M.D. M.S
Medical Oncology, Vanderbilt
Nutrition
Integrative Medicine

BRUCE A. SCHMIDT

From my chair

A PSYCHOTHERAPIST
REVEALS PRACTICAL TOOLS
TO TAKE CHARGE OF
YOUR MENTAL HEALTH

From My Chair
A Psychotherapist Reveals Practical Tools To Take Charge Of Your Mental Health
Bruce A. Schmidt

Published by Mindful Press, St. Louis, MO
Copyright ©2024 Bruce A. Schmidt
All rights reserved.

No part of this publication may be reproduced, stored in a retrieval system, or transmitted in any form or by any means, electronic, mechanical, photocopying, recording, scanning, or otherwise, except as permitted under Section 107 or 108 of the 1976 United States Copyright Act, without the prior written permission of the Publisher. Requests to the Publisher for permission should be addressed to the Permissions Department, Mindful Press, mindfulpress1@gmail.com. Names, characters, businesses, places, events, and incidents are either the products of the author's imagination or used in a fictitious manner. Any resemblance to actual persons, living or dead, or actual events is purely coincidental.

The product information and advice provided (in this book) are intended for general informational purposes only. The author and publisher of this book have made every effort to ensure that the content is accurate and up-to-date at the time of publication. However, they make no representations or warranties of any kind, express or implied, about the completeness, accuracy, reliability, suitability, or availability of the information, products, or services contained in this book for any purpose.

Project Management and Book Design: Davis Creative, LLC, dba: Davis CreativePublishing.com

Publisher's Cataloging-in-Publication
(Provided by Cassidy Cataloguing Services, Inc.)

Names: Schmidt, Bruce A., author.

Title: From my chair / a psychotherapist reveals practical tools to take charge of your mental health / Bruce A. Schmidt.

Description: St. Louis, MO : Mindful Press, [2024]

Identifiers: ISBN: 979-8-9906288-0-9 (paperback) | 979-8-9906288-1-6 (ebook) | LCCN: 2024910096

Subjects: LCSH: Psychotherapy. | Mental health. | Self-actualization (Psychology) | Adjustment (Psychology) | Self-help groups. | Stress management. | LCGFT: Self-help publications. | BISAC: SELF-HELP / General. | SELF-HELP / Personal Growth / Happiness. | BODY, MIND & SPIRIT / Inspiration & Personal Growth.

Classification: LCC: RC480 .S36 2024 | DDC: 616.8914--dc23

ATTENTION CORPORATIONS, UNIVERSITIES, COLLEGES, AND PROFESSIONAL ORGANIZATIONS: Quantity discounts are available on bulk purchases of this book for educational, gift purposes, or as premiums for increasing magazine subscriptions or renewals. Special books or book excerpts can also be created to fit specific needs. For information, please contact Eric Axelbaum, Mindful Press, mindfulpress1@gmail.com.

Dedication

I could not have written this book without the assistance, talents, and friendship of Eric Axelbaum. Thanks to my family, colleagues, patients, and friends, who taught me everything.

> *Peace begins with a smile.*
> — Mother Teresa

TABLE OF CONTENTS

Preface	1
Notes	3
SECTION 1: Let's Get Started	5
Joe At His Workplace	9
Do I Have Depression?	11
Do I Need A Therapist?	21
SECTION 2: Why in the Heck Do I Need a Therapist?	29
Introduction To Integrative Mental Health	31
1 Talk Therapy	35
2 Journaling	39
3 Hydration	43
4 Nutrition	47
5 Exercise	51
6 Sleep	55
7 Complementary Therapies	59
8 Meditation	63
9 Yoga	69
10 Humor	77
11 Hobbies	79
12 Socializing With Intent	83
13 Support Groups	87
14 Finding Purpose	91
15 Reframing Your Mindset	95

16 Practicing Forgiveness	99
17 Self-Compassion	105
18 Setting Boundaries	115
19 Asking For Help	119
20 Medication	123
Closing	**129**
Resources	**131**
About The Author	**135**

Preface

I am pleased to present this guide to you, my dear patients. I have created this simple, interactive, problem-solving workbook to help you thrive with or without my presence. The information and exercises will assist you in obtaining skills to strengthen your emotional well-being and, in some cases, eliminate your mental health issues.

Medical professionals can use this guide to access other mental health solutions for their patients. It will give medical providers another mental health resource.

Finally, I hope you find peace, connection, energy, light, love, and whatever else you seek. In a perfect world, no one would need my services. I would rejoice if this ever happened. In the meantime, I am here if you need me, and so is this booklet.

We need nothing and have everything.
— Bruce

Notes

QUOTES BY BRUCE

My quotes are dispersed throughout this book and appear with my image. You may recognize some of these if you have spent time with me. Please take a moment and reflect on my words. Hopefully, they will help you gain a deeper understanding of the material.

QUOTES BY OTHERS

Other quotes are scattered throughout and appear with the quotation symbol shown here. Take a moment and reflect on these quotes, as they may help you connect more deeply with the information presented.

BRUCE'S FAVORITE PASTIMES/RECIPES

As mentioned throughout this book, one of the keys to good mental health is to occupy yourself with positive, joyful activities. Some of my favorites include spending time with my grandchildren, meditating, gardening, working with Partnership Ethiopia, journaling, and exercising (albeit, I need more). And cooking. I can't get enough of cooking. I love preparing delicious snacks when I need a little pick-me-up. I have included the recipes for six of my favorite dishes. If it cheers you up, try making some of them. While preparing these "feel good" recipes, I encourage you to slow down and "live in the moment." Notice the sounds, sights, smells, tastes, and feelings as you prepare and eat these scrumptious foods. The recipes are sprinkled throughout this manual (look for the cooking pan symbol shown here).

SECTION 1

Let's Get Started

TIPS FOR USING THIS BOOK (A MUST-READ)

The following tips will help make reading this booklet easier:

- While this guide can be an effective tool for people diagnosed with clinical depression, it is not specifically written for them. Instead, it is primarily written for those who feel sad, angry, scared, lonely, jealous, confused, or left out due to environmental or situational events.

- For the sake of this book, I will refer to feeling sad, angry, scared, lonely, jealous, confused, left out, etc., as dealing with "feelings."

- For the sake of this guide, I will refer to those dealing with feelings resulting from a corresponding event as "unsettled" or "upset."

- I will leave the terms "depression" and "anxiety" for the clinical professionals. These terms tend to be misused and may cause people to worry more about their mental health than they should. As a result, I will substitute words like "sad," "upset," "stressed," "troubled," or "worried" in their place.

Don't give all of yourself to anyone. Don't rely on one person for your happiness.
— Bruce

- More important than the terms used is the understanding that these feelings are normal emotions of healthy people. Please read that again. Sadness, anger, and fear (among others) are normal emotions of healthy people, especially when they follow a stressful event.

- So why do some unsettled folks seem happier than others? The answer to that, my friend, is the essence of this book.

- Each integrative health method discussion and workbook activity (section 2) has been kept to a page or two. My goal is to pique your interest. Please investigate the strategies that resonate with you more deeply.

- Changing your mindset is mentioned frequently in this manual. For example, on page 17, I encourage readers to reprogram their brain from focusing on negative feelings to positive ones. In the mental health world, your mindset is how you look at and then deal with personal challenges. Remember, you always have a choice in how you view a situation. In her book Mindset, Carol Dweck uses "fixed" and "growth" to explain some of these skills. The best examples of changing your mindset are the well-known proverbs, "Is the glass half full or half empty?" and "When life gives you lemons, make lemonade." Both of these phrases emphasize looking at the positive side of difficulties.

Joe At His Workplace

"Hi, my name is Joe. I've worked at XYZ Corporation for four years. I write engaging curricula for students with disabilities. It's a pretty easy job because I have lots of experience in this field and believe in what I am doing. I work in an office with five coworkers. I am the only one who specializes in my particular area. My boss is the owner. She shows up at the office for an hour or so every day and often pokes her head into my office, saying "hello" or giving me a directive that often doesn't make sense. I don't usually ask for clarification because she will roll her eyes and mutter something if I do. These incidents bother me a little, but only for a short period.

Lately, I have been experiencing low mood, tension, and sadness more often. I am worried I might have depression, and I am considering contacting my doctor to see if she thinks I should begin taking antidepressant drugs. I have felt this way for about a month. The most recent stressor happened when my boss criticized me in front of the other staff for something that wasn't my fault. That was almost two weeks ago. It was over a minor customer service incident. I let it go because the issue didn't affect my job security. Also, when my coworkers defend themselves from her criticism, it escalates into more trouble than it is worth. Besides, my job is going well, and I feel lucky I don't have to put up with all the office drama my friends seem to have. I have it pretty good here. So why am I feeling low?"

Does Joe need to be medicated? No. Granted, I have the benefit of hindsight. Joe incorrectly assumed that because the last incident was two weeks ago, it couldn't possibly be the reason for his low mood that day. Further, Joe convinced himself that these minor incidents shouldn't bother him. As a result, he didn't deal with them, but his boss' arrival that day triggered those suppressed feelings. Even when months passed between incidents, it stirred up his emotions every time she arrived. He assumed he had depression, and while medication may have helped in the short run, it wouldn't have solved his periodic low moods. So, is Joe suffering from (clinical) depression? No, Joe is an average person dealing with a typical problem.

This book is not about clinical depression, but I want you to understand the difference between depression and the situational low moods depicted in the above example.

If you want it to happen, open that channel yourself. If you want people to treat you with more kindness, be kinder. If you want people to be more open-minded to your views, be more open-minded to theirs.

— Bruce

Do I Have Depression?

Depression, sometimes called *major depressive disorder,* is a medical illness that adversely affects how a person feels, thinks, and acts. It only affects about 1 in 15 adults annually and only 1 in 6 people during their lifetime. Fortunately, it is also treatable.

Depression causes a person to feel sad and lose interest in activities they once enjoyed. It also causes other emotional problems and sometimes physical problems. It decreases one's ability to function at work and at home.

For the sake of this manual, the most essential characteristic of clinical depression is that it usually occurs *without* a corresponding event.

Darkness cannot drive out darkness; only light can do that. Hate cannot drive out hate; only love can do that.
— Martin Luther King, Jr.

If you are concerned about clinical depression, the first step is to see your family physician or mental health practitioner. Talk about your concerns. Request a thorough evaluation. The following is a quick screening for clinical depression.

Depression symptoms vary from minor to severe and can include:

- Feeling sad without a corresponding event

- Loss of interest or pleasure in activities that you once enjoyed

- Changes in appetite (weight loss or gain unrelated to dieting)

- Trouble sleeping or sleeping too much

- Loss of energy or increased fatigue

- Increase in fidgeting (inability to sit still, pacing, handwringing)

- Slowed movements or speech (that are noticed by others)

- Feeling worthless or guilty

- Difficulty thinking, concentrating, or making decisions

- Thoughts of death or suicide

To be diagnosed with clinical depression, one must experience several conditions above for at least two weeks. Also, there must be a change in the level of functioning. Depression is among the most treatable of mental disorders. Between 80 and 90 percent of people with depression respond well to treatment.

DEPRESSION IS DIFFERENT THAN NORMAL WAVES OF EMOTION

We are starting to distinguish between clinical depression and the typical wave of emotions that people experience. What are events that cause people to feel unsettled? Typically, the most stressful ones are:

- The death of a loved one
- Loss of a job
- Declining health
- Ending or conflict in a relationship

However, other less apparent triggers may cause the same feelings. Remember Joe? (If helpful, reread pages 9-10.) These triggers can be so subtle we don't even recognize them when they cause us to feel unsettled. These less intense incidents may also cause the same feelings as the more intense ones. Moreover, these situational feelings, not to be confused with clinical depression, can be addressed in various ways.

It is usual for feelings to develop in response to these stressors. Often, patients experiencing these emotions describe themselves as being "depressed." However, feeling sad, angry, or scared because of a stressor (trigger) is not the same as being clinically depressed. Both types of patients may feel intense sadness and withdrawal from usual activities. However, they are different in important ways:

- In unsettled or upset people, sadness, anger, or fear comes in waves. In clinical depression, the low mood usually lasts longer without a corresponding event.

- In unsettled people, self-esteem is usually maintained.

- In depression, feelings of worthlessness are common.

- In upset people, thoughts of death may surface when thinking of the incidents that caused the low feelings.

- In depression, thoughts of death are present due to feeling worthless or being unable to cope with the pain of depression.

Distinguishing between unsettled and clinically depressed people is critical and can assist patients in getting the appropriate help, support, or treatment they need. As a reminder, this book aims to help those upset folks manage the inevitable and common "lows" of all humans.

Being happy doesn't mean that everything is perfect. It means that you've decided to look beyond the imperfections.

— Gerard Way

REFRAMING YOUR MINDSET/REPRESSED FEELINGS

Sometimes, we think we are the only ones suffering from the "low" moments mentioned above. If you scroll through Facebook, Instagram, Twitter, Snapchat, or any other social media platform, you may get the impression that everyone is happy-go-lucky, in love, and always "up." However, most people don't choose to share their unsettled or low moments with the public. Unfortunately, this censorship of reality perpetuates the idea that struggling is abnormal when it is a large part of every person's life.

The following statistics are not universal or documented; they represent the clients who have gravitated to me through the years.

Based on the observations of literally thousands of patients I have seen over the past 40 years, I estimate a typical person lives on the low end of the emotional spectrum (mad, sad, nervous) about 50 percent of the time and in the moderate zone approximately 30 percent of the time. If you are decent at math, you realize they exist only about 20 percent of the time in the high end (happy, relaxed). Does this surprise you? Do you feel better knowing other people often live in these average to low periods, too? If you are struggling, I hope it helps you realize how normal you are.

However, we aren't going to dwell on how miserable everyone is. Let's focus on:

- Managing these feelings
- Placing them in the right frame of mind
- Handling or accepting them when they arise
- Training your mind to focus on feelings of happiness, contentment, pleasure, bliss, joy, peace, love, and fun

It takes effort to reprogram your brain from focusing on the negative feelings to concentrating on the positive ones. Let's start with recognizing and reframing low moments. I encourage you to first sit with the emotion. Try it on. Let it do its thing. Don't fight it or deny it. While doing this, slowly start trying to connect the emotion to the situation that may be causing it. Here are some possibilities to consider:

What's bothering me? Have any of the following occurred lately?

- Death or illness of a friend or family member
- Loss or change in job
- Declining health
- Ending of a relationship
- Conflict with friends or family members
- Upsetting local, national, or global news stories
- A personal situation that didn't work out as you had hoped

However, other less apparent triggers may cause the same feelings. They are so subtle that you may not even recognize them when they occur. As a side note, sometimes healthy people's moods change without a corresponding event. Why? While the human brain is a biological marvel, it is still an unpredictable and mysterious machine. Nevertheless, the primary reason for these low moments is that people have suppressed feelings that may be triggered by stimuli they don't understand or are not aware of when they occur. Reread the last sentence.

When you find the connection between the feeling and the cause, try to recognize the specific word and reason for the feeling. For example:

- I am *nervous* about my upcoming doctor's appointment.
- I am *angry* at Jeff because he told Mary something private about me.
- I am *scared* about my job interview. I worry I will forget the answers I have practiced.

Don't analyze or judge it; recognize it. In this way, you will have to reflect on the reason for the reaction. Eventually, identifying the trigger of your feelings will allow you to deal with it directly and do something about it. For example, many of my patients recognize their stress is related to a recent encounter with a family member, friend, or coworker. It hasn't gone away because they haven't allowed themselves to feel, process, or respond. It takes on a life more dramatic than it should. In hindsight, many of my patients said the situation wasn't essential or traumatic, but ignoring it (intentionally or not) made it worse than it needed to be.

In the book *Healing Back Pain*, one of Dr. John Sarno's premises is that repressed feelings cause most chronic back, hip, neck, and shoulder pains. Even the most educated and successful people are guilty of repressing their emotions. Dr. Sarno further maintains that people are structured so their bodies are willing to take on incredible physical pains to mask their emotional distress. In much the same way, you may feel intense sadness without knowing what is causing it. Therapy appointments, journaling, etc., may help keep those repressed emotions to a minimum.

If you are depressed, you are living in the past; if you are anxious, you are living in the future; if you are at peace, you are living in the present.

— Lao Tzu

The world doesn't owe you anything.
No person owes you anything.
Not your spouse, children, parents, friends, employees, etc.

— Bruce

Do I Need A Therapist?

In talk therapy (aka psychotherapy), the patient is encouraged to discuss previous traumas and other pertinent issues with their therapist. The main goals of talk therapy are processing, treating, and resolving mental health conditions.

Psychotherapy may involve just one patient, but it can include others. For example, family or couples therapy can help address issues within these close relationships. Group therapy brings together people with similar problems in a supportive environment and can help the person learn how others cope in similar situations.

Private sessions typically last anywhere from 30 minutes to an hour and cost anywhere from $25 per session (with insurance copay) to $250 per hour. In my 40 years of practice,

I have learned, above all, that people need to have someone with whom they can:

- Tell their deepest and darkest secrets
- Express anger and sadness
- Share their joys
- Be themselves
- Feel supported
- Be connected

A therapist can help with all of the above. Do people need therapy? Do you see a dentist even if you don't have a cavity? Of course. Preventive maintenance is the key to good physical and mental health. So, it doesn't hurt to enlist a mental health professional to talk to before times get tough or for preventative maintenance. There may be times when you need the help of a professional therapist more, so don't wait until life gets too hectic before finding that right person. Having a therapist doesn't mean you have clinical depression or are mentally ill.

CHOOSING THE RIGHT THERAPIST

These tips can help you find the right therapist.

- Ask your family doctor.
- Do a little research on the internet.

- Are they close enough that traveling there isn't a burden? For most people, that means within 15 minutes each way. What is your limit?

- Do they provide telehealth or virtual sessions? (Discussed in section 2.)

- Contact family and friends.
    - You can't put enough emphasis on word of mouth.
    - Who do the people you connect with recommend?
    - Why do they like them? "They are nice" isn't a good enough reason.
    - What are their strengths and challenges?
    - How available are they?
    - Are they discreet?

- If you have a specific issue (e.g., addiction, Parkinson's disease, body image, intimacy), contact that organization or support group and ask for recommendations. I have a client who tragically lost her daughter to drug addiction. She found a therapist specializing in grief therapy for survivors of loved ones with drug addiction. Finding the right therapist may take a little more time and energy. And just like relationships, there is more than one right therapist.

RECIPE 1: HONEY BUTTER BISCUITS

Chef Bruce says, "Buttery and flaky, these melt-in-the-mouth biscuits are my favorite Southern comfort food. For a tasty variation, add ½ cup of shredded sharp cheddar cheese to the dough."

Prep Time: 15 minutes
Total Time: 30 minutes
Yield: 8–12 biscuits

Ingredients:

- 2 1/2 cups flour, plus more as needed
- 1 tablespoon baking powder
- 1 1/2 teaspoons salt
- 8 tablespoons (1 stick) unsalted *frozen* butter
- 4 tablespoons (1/2 stick) unsalted *softened* butter
- 3/4 cup *chilled* buttermilk
- 3 tablespoons honey

For even fluffier biscuits, place one stick of butter (8 tablespoons) and mixing bowl in the freezer for at least an hour before making the dough. Also, make sure to chill the buttermilk.

Directions:

1. Preheat oven to 400°F. Line a greased baking sheet with parchment paper.

2. Combine the flour, baking powder, and salt in a large bowl.

3. Use a pastry cutter to cut the *frozen* butter (1 stick) into the mixture until it forms coarse crumbs.

4. Mix together the buttermilk and honey in a bowl. Make a well in the center of the flour mixture and add the liquid mixture. Stir until just combined; do not overmix.

5. Lightly flour a work surface and turn the dough out. Press it gently until it's about an inch thick. Fold it and gently flatten again. Repeat this three to four times.

6. Use a biscuit cutter or a floured glass to cut out biscuits. Don't twist as you push straight down—this will make sure your biscuits rise properly. Place the biscuits on the baking sheet. Bake for about 15 minutes or until golden brown.

7. While baking the biscuits, combine the *softened* butter (1/2 stick) with honey in a small bowl and stir until smooth. Brush the warm biscuits with the honey butter before serving.

Inspired by the Honey Butter Biscuits recipe on blackpeoplesrecipes.com.

RECIPE 2: GREEK SALAD

Chef Bruce says, "Sure, the Greek salad is wholesome and nutritious, but it packs an 'oomph' for your tastebuds! It is flexible; you can modify the ingredients to your taste."

Prep Time: 15 minutes
Total Time: 20 minutes
Yield: 3 entrees or 6 side servings

Ingredient Choices (choose the ingredients you like):

- Fruits: Figs, kalamata olives, black olives, cherry tomatoes
- Veggies: 1 red onion, 1 cucumber, 1 green bell pepper, 3 or 4 pepperoncini peppers
- Lettuce: 1 head romaine lettuce (5 or 6 cups, 1.25 to 1.50 pounds)
- Grains: Pita bread, croutons
- Protein: Ham, lamb, Genoa salami
- Dairy: Crumbled feta cheese, shredded Parmesan cheese
- Dressing: 3 oz. olive oil, 1 oz. red wine vinegar, dash of lemon juice, and a pinch of garlic, oregano, salt, and pepper

Directions:

1. Wash and rinse the fresh fruits, vegetables, and lettuce.

2. Halve the olives and cherry tomatoes if desired (you may prefer to keep them whole).

3. Chop the red onions, cucumbers, and both types of peppers.

4. Tear or cut the lettuce; tearing by hand takes longer but may deliver a better taste. Fill a large salad bowl with the fresh, clean, dry lettuce.

5. Slowly pour the olive oil over the lettuce, followed by the vinegar, lemon juice, and spices. Mix with clean hands or salad tongs.

6. Add fruits, veggies, proteins, and dairy. Mix with the lettuce.

7. Add croutons or pita bread last.

For an even healthier/lower-calorie version:

- Use croutons and pita bread made from whole-grain wheat.
- Use lots of fruits and vegetables.
- Use meats, salad dressing, and cheese in moderation.

Source: Eric Axelbaum and Bruce A. Schmidt

SECTION 2

Why in the Heck Do I Need a Therapist?

Introduction To Integrative Mental Health

Integrative health combines mainstream (conventional or Western) and alternative (holistic or Eastern) medicines. There are several actions people can take to help deal with their low moments. For many clients, regular exercise helps create positive feelings and improves mood. Getting enough sleep, eating a healthy diet, and avoiding excessive alcohol (a depressant) can also help reduce unsettled periods.

In this section, I have included 20 practices that may help you along your journey to obtain better mental health. As you glance over these habits, be mindful of the following:

- You likely will only be interested in employing some of the 20 methods.

- You may have already considered or attempted a handful of them.

- Pick the methods that resonate with you and then complete the accompanying exercise. I have provided some space to jot notes; however, you may prefer to have a notebook or digital device available for that purpose.

- Select three to seven health methods that interest you and implement two to five.

- Each integrative health method discussion and activity has been kept to a minimum. My goal is to pique your interest. Please further investigate the strategies that resonate with you more deeply.

- The following section provides initiatives that may benefit your mental health. While none is considered risky, I recommend you consult a medical professional before beginning any new program geared around exercise, nutrition, or medication. These include, but are not limited to, routines 3–9 and 20 listed on the next page.

BRUCE'S TOP 20 INTEGRATIVE MENTAL HEALTH ROUTINES

1. Talk Therapy
2. Journaling
3. Hydration
4. Nutrition
5. Exercise
6. Sleep
7. Complementary Therapies
8. Meditation
9. Yoga
10. Humor
11. Hobbies
12. Socializing with Intent
13. Support Group
14. Finding Purpose
15. Reframing Your Mindset
16. Practicing Forgiveness
17. Self-Compassion
18. Setting Boundaries
19. Asking for Help
20. Medication

A summary of each habit, along with a corresponding exercise, follows.

1
Talk Therapy

For a more detailed account of talk therapy, see Section 1 ("Do I Need a Therapist?"). Talk therapy is one strategy for achieving overall good mental health. It may be a good starting point for someone becoming aware of increased stress. As mentioned, it is a good idea to engage the services of a therapist before you desperately need one.

One silver lining to the pandemic we endured in 2020 is the mainstreaming of telehealth. Engaging with medical professionals via virtual communication is no longer considered ineffective. Zoom, FaceTime, or audio chatting can have the same benefits as face-to-face interactions. Of course, each individual may differ in his or her preference.

Like anything else, you will get out of it what you put into it. I have noticed traits such as honesty, openness, transparency, accountability, vulnerability, and respect in my more successful patients. Be yourself, and don't fear going out of your comfort zone.

The two Ls: lonely and love. You need both to be happy. Think about this: Could you feel or understand happiness if you never felt sadness?"

— Bruce

Let it hurt. Let it heal. Let it go."

— Unknown

EXERCISE 1: FINDING A THERAPIST

If finding a therapist is vital to you, consider the following:

- List the issues that concern you about your mental health.

- Ask your family, friends, and doctor for the best-suited therapists.

- Find out if your health insurance pays for counseling.

- Do a little online research on therapists in your area. Consider the following items:
    - The maximum distance you are willing to travel to see a therapist
    - Are you okay with telehealth sessions?

- If you have a specific issue, contact that organization or support group and ask for recommendations.

The goal of this exercise is not necessarily to begin counseling; it's just the first step in deciding if therapy is right for you. Finding the right therapist and participating in a session can never hurt.

2
Journaling

Dealing with emotions can be difficult, but journaling may help more than you imagine. It is well-documented that writing down thoughts, ideas, and questions is much more effective than just thinking about them. The following tips may help you get started with journaling:

- Use a paper journal or a digital journal (laptop, smartphone, tablet).

- Write daily, if possible, or whenever you need to.

- Keep your journal in a convenient place (unless you are worried about security).

- Don't worry about grammar or spelling.

- There are several formats you might use (bullet points, songs, drawings, letters, etc.).

- Make your journal a judgment-free zone.

- Don't hold back; express whatever is on your mind.

- Try to release negative emotions (anger, sadness, fear, etc.).

- Periodically, reread what you have written.

- Keep track of your symptoms if you are working through a difficult period. You might rate your mental health that day from 1 to 10. Compare these ratings to the day's activities to see if there is a correlation between your stressors and your mood.

What you think of yourself is much more important than what people think of you!"
— Seneca

EXERCISE 2: JOURNALING

If journaling sounds helpful to you, review the guidance shared here and start writing, keyboarding, or texting.

3
Hydration

Hydration is essential, whether you are intensely active or primarily sedentary. Hydration is simply drinking the right amount of water or appropriate fluids to enable your cells, tissues, and organs to function. (Some foods provide water as well.) If your body is low on fluids, it can't work well.

Check your urine. If you are well hydrated, it will be colorless or light yellow. It will be dark yellow or yellow-orange if you are dehydrated.

For most people, water is all that is needed. You may substitute low- or zero-caffeinated beverages for water. Unfortunately, there are only a few *healthy* options. I make a decaf iced tea or put enough cranberry juice in water to enjoy the taste. Juices don't have caffeine but may contain high amounts of sugar. Caffeinated drinks, like soda or coffee, are not your best bets for effective hydration.

Consider sports drinks if you exercise at a high intensity or it is very hot. The calories, potassium, and other nutrients help you perform better and recover quicker. Unfortunately, they are high in sodium and calories, so don't overdo it. Some may have caffeine, which may cause dehydration later.

Hydration improves your mood; dehydration impairs your mood. Drinking more water daily is a painless way to better mental health.

The old cardinal rule states that adults should drink six to eight cups of water daily.

A more precise calculation is:
Body weight x 0.50 = ounces of water per day

Therefore, a 150-pound person should consume about 75 ounces (9–10 cups) of water daily.

Recent studies indicate that drinking 10–16 cups a day is preferable. Of course, this depends on many factors (heat, exercise, weight, health, gender, age). The above recommendations cover fluids from water and other beverages. However, about 20 percent of daily fluid intake may come from fruits and vegetables such as strawberries and broccoli; therefore, the amount you drink may be tempered somewhat.

Your doctor is also a good source for this information.

EXERCISE 3: HYDRATION

If you feel you are not adequately hydrated, consider the following:

- How many ounces or cups (millimeters or liters) of water do you consume in a typical day? If you are unsure, monitor your consumption for a day or two.

- If you decide to increase your consumption, how do you plan on implementing it? How many cups per day is your goal?

- Try your plan for a week. How did it go? Can you sustain it? If not, try something else.

4

Nutrition

Good nutrition refers to consuming the right types and proper amounts of foods. There are three basic nutrition guidelines:

Guideline 1
Eating foods from all five groups (see examples below) is essential because different groups have additional nutrients your body needs. For example, even though vegetables are very healthy, if that is all you ever ate, you would be missing the other vital nutrients different food groups provide.

Examples of the Five Food Groups

Fruits	Veggies	Grains	Protein	Dairy
Apples Bananas Kiwis Mangoes Grapes	Carrots Broccoli Asparagus Green beans Bell peppers	Quinoa Pretzels Bread Rice Crackers	Eggs Lean meats Fish Nuts/Seeds Beans	Milk Butter Cheese Yogurt Cottage cheese

Guideline 2

Not only do you want to eat foods from all five groups, but you also want to eat *various* foods within each group. For example, if you love bananas, you should still eat other fruits to obtain nutrients not found in bananas.

Guideline 3

Consuming the right amount of all types of food is essential. Even if you eat various foods from all the food groups, you still have to eat the right amounts. Eating too much or too little will not give you proper nutrition.

Besides the physical reasons for good nutrition—such as stronger bones, muscles, heart, brain, and sleep—eating right also gives you more energy and can make you happier.

It's always a good idea to check with your doctor or dietician before starting a new eating regimen. Furthermore, if you have diabetes, follow the diet prescribed by your medical professional.

EXERCISE 4: NUTRITION

If you are interested in better nutrition, consider the following questions:

- How would you rate your nutrition on a scale from 1 (worst) to 10 (best)? If your rating was above 7, consider skipping this exercise.

- What areas of your nutrition need the most work?

- Besides contacting a nutritionist, what else can you do immediately?

- How will you monitor your improvement? Here are some options:
    - Waist size
    - Weight
    - Energy level
    - Body Mass Index
    - Other

5
Exercise

Exercise generally means any movement that makes your muscles work and your body burn calories. The benefits can be broken down into four categories.

Inside Your Body

Exercise helps almost every part of your body. It builds strong bones. It helps your muscles grow and reduces injury. Regular exercise helps your heart, lungs, digestion, circulation, and brain. It pushes blood and oxygen to your brain.

The Appearance of Your Body

Regular exercise enables you to burn more calories, even when not exercising. Exercise helps you maintain a healthy weight or lose weight. It also helps your body look leaner and more athletic.

Mental

Exercise creates new brain cells, which increases your brain's ability to think and solve problems. It also prevents mental decline and memory loss by strengthening the part of the brain that is responsible for memory and learning.

Emotional/Mood

Consistent exercise will improve your mood and lessen feelings of sadness and stress. The intensity or type of exercise doesn't matter. Exercise changes the part of the brain that regulates mood. Physical activity also helps you sleep and relax better, resulting in better moods.

Fitness Program Components

A well-rounded fitness or exercise program will include the following.

- STRENGTH TRAINING

  The basic idea of strength training is you exercise a muscle or group of muscles until they are tired. At this point, the muscles start to break down. As they recover over the next few days, they become stronger.

- CARDIOVASCULAR

  Cardiovascular or aerobic exercises, like jogging or swimming, strengthen the heart and lungs. They may be performed longer but with less intensity.

- STRETCHING

  Stretching is the process of lengthening the muscles and connective soft tissues. It will improve your flexibility and the range of motion around your joints. The importance of stretching increases substantially as we age.

EXERCISE 5: EXERCISE

If you feel you are not getting enough exercise, consider the following questions:

- How would you rate your fitness on a scale of 1 (worst) to 10 (best)? If your rating is above 7, consider skipping this exercise.

- What areas of your fitness routine need the most work?

- Besides contacting a fitness trainer, what else can you do immediately?

- How will you monitor your improvement? Here are some options:
    - Waist size
    - Weight
    - Energy level
    - Body Mass Index
    - Strength
    - Body-fat percentage
    - Other

Don't forget to contact your physician before starting any new fitness routine.

6
Sleep

It's no secret that sleep and mental health are closely connected. Read the following information about sleeping:

- Adults need between seven and nine hours of sleep a night.

- During sleep, many bodily functions recharge or heal: brain, mood, memory, creativity, energy, thinking, weight management, and the operation of body systems.

- Not getting enough sleep may cause hyperactivity, aggressiveness, difficulty getting along with others, bad moods, trouble controlling emotions, and anxiety.

- Refrain from exercising rigorously, eating a heavy meal, drinking excessively, using technology, or consuming caffeine too close to bedtime. Caffeine is in many products besides coffee: chocolate, ice cream, cereal, pudding, hot cocoa, chocolate chip cookies, chocolate milk, yogurt, protein bars, soda, and mints.

- Keep your bedroom cool, dark, clean, and quiet. Avoid late-night studying. Try reading, taking a warm bath, meditating, listening to music, relaxing, or breathing deeply right before bedtime—just one or two, not all.

- Set a regular bedtime and wake-up time. Limit weekend catch-up sleep to one hour.

EXERCISE 6: SLEEP

If you believe you are not getting enough sleep, consider the following questions:

- How would you rate your sleep on a scale of 1 (worst) to 10 (best)? If your rating was above 7, consider skipping the rest of the exercise.

- What are the reasons you are having trouble sleeping?

- Besides contacting a medical professional (a sleep-disorder doctor), what else can you do immediately?

- How will you monitor your improvement? Consider these options:
    - Number of hours of sleep per night
    - How you wake up feeling
    - Energy during the day
    - Snoring

7
Complementary Therapies

Everyone deals with stress. It becomes locked as tension in various body sections, including your brain. People who deal positively with stress are much happier and healthier. One of these complementary therapies may lighten your mind, body, and spirit.

Massage
People perceive massage therapy as mainly for the physical body, but the psychological benefits are equally valuable. It helps you release tension in your mind, increase awareness, get better sleep, and lower anxiety. Physically, it causes the body to release the hormone oxytocin, which facilitates bonding and, in some cases, even prevents stress. Also, massage can help free endorphins, the feel-good hormone released by the body in times of joy and happiness.

Aroma

Inhaling the scents of specific oils can elicit profound emotional responses to help you uplift your spirits, find comfort and balance, or ease anxiety. There are many types of essential oils. They can be used for various physical and emotional wellness applications. For example, peppermint oil can alleviate upset stomachs, while lavender oil is known for its calming effects. Because the aromatic molecules in essential oils directly access the limbic area (emotional seat of the brain), smell is the fastest way to affect mood.

Floating

Floating is an excellent alternative for individuals looking for a natural approach to healing. Floatation therapy in a saltwater tank shields you from external distractions. This helps your mind relax and focus on reaching a calmer state. Floating can significantly reduce anxiety, depression, and other mental health conditions like attention-deficit hyperactivy disorder, stress, and post-traumatic stress disorder. It releases gravity's hold on the body while giving the mind time to relax fully.

Sound Therapy

One study published in the *Journal of Evidence-Based Integrative Medicine* found that a one-hour sound meditation session helped people reduce tension, anger, fatigue, and depression while increasing a sense of spiritual harmony. Sound therapy is more than just listening to music. It involves sound-wave vibration. A sound bath uses Tibetan singing bowls, quartz bowls, and bells to direct the listener.

EXERCISE 7: COMPLEMENTARY THERAPIES

- Which, if any, of the above complementary therapies have you tried? If you have tried one, what is your interest in pursuing that one again?

- How about the therapies you have not tried? Any interest? Which one(s)? Why?

- How practical is adopting one of the complementary therapies into your weekly routine? Consider distance, cost, time, and other factors.

- If you are interested, investigate one or two options this week.

8
Meditation

Meditation has been a tradition in Eastern cultures for thousands of years. It is still practiced in China and many other places worldwide. Meditation is a way of becoming more present, calm, and empathetic. It helps bring your awareness into the present moment. When you meditate, you purposely set aside all chatter in your mind so you can focus on the present (your body, your breath, your environment). Meditation helps in the moments you are practicing it and when you are not. In Buddhist philosophy, the goal of meditation is to free the mind of things it cannot control, such as external events or strong emotions.

There are many ways to practice meditation. None are right, wrong, or better than the others. Generally, here are the steps:

- Sit, lie, or stand in a comfortable position.

- Close your eyes.

- Begin breathing naturally and easily.

- Focus on your breath as it flows in and out of your body.

- If a random thought enters your mind, accept it, then gently let it go.

- Continue breathing, relaxing, and clearing your mind for a specific amount of time.

Emotional Benefits

- Decreases worry, anxiety, impulsivity, stress, fear, loneliness, and depression.

- Increases self-esteem, self-acceptance, optimism, relaxation, awareness, and mood.

- Prevents overeating, smoking, nail-biting, and other nervous habits.

- Increases concrete thinking, creative thinking, problem-solving, memory, recall, focus, and decision-making.

One small positive thought in the morning can change your whole day.
— Unknown

EXERCISE 8: MEDITATION

- Meditate for 2 minutes a day. That's it. Do this for a week, then try 4 minutes daily for another week or two. Add about 2 minutes a day until you get to 10 or 15 minutes a day. Finally, practice meditation as it fits in your lifestyle and needs.

- Do it first thing every morning.

- Don't worry about how you do it. Just do it. Sit. Stand. Lie. Pillow or no pillow. Just do it.

- Ask yourself how you are feeling. How does your body feel? Your mind? Your emotions? Are you tired? Nervous? Whatever it is, it is okay.

- Try it right now. Find a comfortable place to sit. Turn your attention to your breath. While inhaling slowly, follow your breath through your nose to your lungs. Try counting "one" as you inhale the first breath, then "two" as you slowly exhale. Repeat this 10 times.

- Your mind will wander. Everyone's does. When you notice it wandering, relax and gently return to your breathing.

- When random thoughts enter your mind, look at them positively, then gently allow them to leave.

- If thoughts or feelings do arise, let them stay. Allow them to be present. Don't try to analyze them or figure them out. Feel the emotion.

- Try this occasionally. It's called a body scan. Focus your attention on one body part at a time. Start at your feet. How do they feel? Slowly move up to your ankles and so on.

- You can meditate almost anywhere: in your office, bedroom, park, plane, train, or elevator. Always put safety first, though. You should never meditate while driving or completing any task that requires your full attention.

- Smile when done. Be grateful that you had the time to do this by yourself.

BRUCE'S FAVORITE MEDITATION RECIPE

- Make hot tea with full attention.
- Sip slowly with intention.
- Take two deep breaths between each sip.
- Love yourself and all that exists.

Love, joy, and peace cannot flourish until you have freed yourself from mind dominance."

— Eckhart Tolle

9
Yoga

Yoga is one of the oldest disciplines known. It originated in India thousands of years ago. One translation of the word "yoga" is to join or unite. This makes sense because uniting the body, mind, and spirit is the main purpose of yoga.

Modern yoga is most commonly associated with physical postures or asanas, which aim to improve flexibility, strength, balance, and stress release. These postures often combine with controlled breathing techniques to create mindfulness and relaxation. While there are numerous styles of yoga, most of them emphasize the importance of connecting with one's inner self, achieving mental clarity, and promoting physical well-being.

Many benefits of yoga extend beyond the physical realm. Yoga can reduce stress and anxiety, improve sleep quality, and boost emotional well-being. It also helps with focus, which facilitates improved thinking and decision-making. Moreover, it may give people a spiritual connection and purpose, allowing them to explore their inner selves and attain a deeper understanding of life.

Getting started can be as simple as attending a local studio or finding a quiet space, unrolling a yoga mat, and following along with an online class. Yoga is available to individuals of all ages and fitness levels. Whether you are a beginner or an experienced yogi, the key is to be patient, listen to your body, and focus on the journey (rather than trying to be perfect). Yoga's holistic approach can bring balance and serenity to your stressful life.

Satisfaction lies in the effort, not in the attainment."
— Gandhi

EXERCISE 9: YOGA

If you are interested in trying yoga or want to learn more about it, consider responding to the following prompts:

- Have you ever tried or observed a yoga class?

- If so, what do you remember about it?

- What did you like about it?

- What didn't you like about it?

- How close are you to the nearest yoga studio(s)? *Note: YMCAs, community centers, churches, and gyms hold classes, too.*

- If you are still curious, contact a few locations and see if they are right for you. Some factors to consider are age, levels of exertion, proximity, cost, and schedule.

RECIPE 3: SUMMER SUCCOTASH

Chef Bruce says, "If you feel a little blue, have some succotash. Everything is fresh, and it sure hits the spot."

Prep Time: 30 minutes
Total Time: 60 minutes
Yield: 6 servings

Ingredients:

- 2 tablespoons olive oil
- 1 medium red onion, finely chopped
- 1 clove garlic, minced
- 2–3 medium jalapenos, deseeded and finely chopped
- 3 whole carrots, peeled and diced
- 3 stalks celery, diced
- 1/4 cup dry white wine
- 3 whole zucchini, diced
- 4 large ripe tomatoes, diced
- 1 1/2 cups frozen or canned sweet corn OR 2 ears corn on the cob, cut off the cob
- 1 dash Borsari seasoned salt
- 1 cup canned or frozen lima beans (optional)

Directions:

1. When preparing the veggies, the key is to have them all cut to the same size.

2. Add the oil to a pan and sauté the onion, garlic, and jalapenos until the onions are translucent.

3. Add carrots, celery, and white wine.

4. Add zucchini and stir well to cook evenly.

5. Add tomatoes, let everything simmer briefly, then add the corn.

6. Add lima beans (optional).

7. Stir until mixture is incorporated and heated thoroughly.

8. Add Borsari to season.

9. Best served with good crusty bread over pasta as a dinner or as a side companion to grilled chicken, steak, or fish.

Source: Bruce A. Schmidt

RECIPE 4: RUTH WAKEFIELD'S ORIGINAL TOLL HOUSE COOKIES

Chef Bruce says, "This might be my favorite chocolate chip cookie recipe. It's good anytime. Occasionally, I will use macadamia nuts instead of chopped nuts. Adding vanilla or cinnamon ice cream makes for a decadent topping."

Prep Time: 20 minutes
Total Time: 45 minutes
Yield: 2–3 dozen

Ingredients:

- 1 cup unsalted butter, plus more as needed
- 3/4 cup firmly packed light brown sugar
- 3/4 cup granulated sugar
- 2 large eggs, beaten
- 1 teaspoon baking soda
- 1 teaspoon hot water
- 2 1/4 cups all-purpose flour, sifted
- 1 teaspoon salt
- 1 cup chopped nuts or macadamia nuts
- 12 oz. (2 cups) semisweet chocolate chips
- 1 teaspoon vanilla extract

Directions:

1. Preheat oven to 375°F and lightly grease two cookie sheets.

2. Stir together the butter, light brown sugar, and granulated sugar until the mixture looks creamy. Mix in the beaten eggs.

3. Dissolve the baking soda in the hot water, then stir into the mixture.

4. Sift the flour and salt together and add to the butter mixture.

5. Stir in the nuts, chocolate chips, and vanilla.

6. Drop by the tablespoon onto prepared cookie sheets and bake until browned at the edges, 10–12 minutes.

7. Enjoy with ice cream for an even more delicious treat.

Inspired by the original Toll House Cookies, invented by Ruth Wakefield at the Toll House Inn, Whitman, Massachusetts.

10
Humor

Humor takes many forms. One thing we do know is that a good laugh is essential to your mental health. Medical studies have shown that laughter is a natural health remedy and stress reliever.

Laughing does wonders for your insides. A good chuckle improves the intake of oxygen-rich air, stimulating your muscles and organs, such as the heart and lungs.

In terms of good mental health, it causes your brain to release endorphins (hormones that cause feelings of pleasure). Laughter also stimulates rapid blood circulation, which may help calm you.

EXERCISE 10: HUMOR

Everyone can use a little more humor in their lives. If you are interested:

- Try to be involved with activities and people that make you happy or laugh. You don't need to go to a comedy club to achieve this.

- Participate in fun-loving or silly conversations, even if it is out of your comfort zone. Sometimes, the worst attempts at humor are the funniest. Thus, the invention of the bad dad jokes.

- Movies, social media, television, and the internet may generate laughter.

- If you are a little older, like me, be aware that things that used to be funny may be inappropriate or rude now.

- And for extra credit, share your favorite joke or two with a friend or colleague. Don't remember any? Make up one or find one online or in a bookstore.

"When I was younger, my parents sent me to a child psychologist. I don't get why — that kid taught me nothing."

11
Hobbies

Engaging in activities outside your everyday routines may increase energy, lower stress, inspire you, make you more attractive, help you make new friends, generate income, distract you from disturbing thoughts, and act as a form of meditation. Choose enjoyable, affordable, stress-free, meditative, and healthy ones. Still trying to figure out what to do? Here are some hobby ideas:

- Reorganizing your living space
- Painting or photography
- Playing a musical instrument
- Practicing tai chi, yoga, or golf
- Doing arts and crafts

- Engaging in craftsmanship (metal, jewelry, pottery, wood carving, glass blowing)

- Volunteering at a dog shelter, nursing home, or hospital

- Hiking/backpacking

- Kayaking

- Vintage-clothes collecting

- Taking weekend trips (doesn't have to cost much)

- Learning to cook international cuisine (Indian, Thai, French, Greek, Italian)

- Sewing (quilting, crocheting, knitting, embroidery)

- Exploring antique stores and garage sales for hidden treasures and restoring them

- Rock climbing

- Learning to dance (jazz, ballet, ballroom, country, square)

- Upcycling (find unused things around the house and give them a new look and use)

- Playing indoor games (bridge, poker, mahjong, chess, checkers, and other board games)

- Playing fantasy sports

- Wine tasting, visiting wineries, brewing beer, roasting coffee
- Writing letters (this is a lost art)
- Participating in a book club
- Making a scrapbook
- Researching your family tree
- Camping, rafting, fishing, bird watching
- Gardening
- Starting a collection (coins, stamps, trading cards, records, shells, postcards)
- Learning a new language
- Taking up magic, performing for friends
- Joining an investment club
- Participating in or watching local theater
- Putting together puzzles
- Working on cars
- Picking berries or learning about wild edibles
- Doing amusement park activities (batting cage, bumper cars, go-carts, miniature golf)

EXERCISE 11: HOBBIES

If you would like to learn a new hobby, consider the following:

Choose or highlight your favorite hobbies from the above list.

Add any hobbies you want to try that are not on the list.

Remember that some hobbies can start with a simple shopping trip (crafts) while others involve substantial time (new language) or money (collecting coins).

Contact a knowledgeable person, do research, or get started on one of these hobbies.

12
Socializing With Intent

Interacting with others increases feelings of well-being and lowers feelings of sadness, anger, and fear. Social people are less likely to develop dementia than those who are less sociable.

"Socializing with intent" activities may overlap with some of the hobbies covered in the previous pages. Ideally, you will find activities that satisfy both categories. In the same vein, it's a good idea to choose social activities that are both physically and mentally engaging.

An article in the *Atlanta Journal-Constitution* outlines five types of friendships according to psychotherapist Niro Feliciano:

- *Close friends*: These are your "inner circle" friends. You can be authentic and intimate around them.

- *Lifelong friends*: These have staying power because your friendship has grown over many years.

- *Work friends*: These friends keep your spirits up while at work.

- *Convenience friends*: These friendships may be formed, for example, with the parents of your child's friends or people you meet at the gym.

- *Same-chapter friends*: These friendships include people in the same life stage (e.g., college dorm roommates).

Remember to seek socialization opportunities concerning the friendship types above in all five categories.

Give it up and make it happen."
— Bruce

EXERCISE 12: SOCIALIZING WITH INTENT

If you feel you could use an injection of socializing, choose a few of the following ideas and get started:

- Use Skype, Zoom, FaceTime, or social media to catch up with family and friends.

- As you walk through your neighborhood, try to stop and say "hello" to people you meet. It might be easier if you bring a friend or dog along.

- Take a class at your local YMCA, library, or health center.

- Attend religious services and events at your temple, synagogue, or church.

- Volunteer somewhere where like-minded people might attend.

- Go to neighborhood or community functions.

- Play a group sport like pickleball, golf, tennis, or volleyball.

- Join a gym.

- Find a support group (see next category).

- Join a book club.

- Invite friends (new or existing) over for board games or other activities.

- Take a cooking or foreign language class.

Which of the above is most appealing? Why?

As mentioned before, we encourage you to venture outside your comfort zone, but not to be reckless or unsafe.

13
Support Groups

A support group brings together people dealing with everyday challenges like addiction, grief, health issues, gender or sexual orientation issues, and many more. Ideally, a support group will allow you to share your personal experiences; express feelings; learn coping strategies; and acquire first-hand, practical information about your concerns. Group therapy sessions are similar but are overseen by a licensed mental health provider.

There are several ways to find the right support group. For example, you can contact your doctor, nonprofit organizations, friends, family, colleagues, and the websites of national institutions that specialize in the issue.

Some patients worry about a lack of confidentiality, knowing someone else in the group, and being judged. While those are legitimate concerns, most members find these risks somewhat rare and enjoy rich, positive experiences. Of course, if you experience negative encounters, you can leave the group any time.

Other benefits or aspects include:

- You only share what you are comfortable sharing.

- Members often sign confidentiality agreements.

- You develop better coping strategies.

- You can find growth through shared experiences.

- You learn vital, relevant, and practical information about your condition.

- You can maintain a sense of hope.

- You may feel less lonely, isolated, or judged.

- You can make new friends with people experiencing similar issues.

- You seldom see someone you know (you can decide if it is a problem or not).

You will get the most from a support group if you:

- Take positive risks.

- Share your feelings and experiences.

- Be open-minded to other's views, suggestions, and experiences.

Be a triple threat:
1) give love,
2) volunteer, and
3) make a difference.
— Bruce

We are just walking each other home.
— Ram Dass

EXERCISE 13: SUPPORT GROUPS

If participating in a support group intrigues you, consider the following:

- First, of course, determine what kind of support group you are seeking. The right support group may be evident for some readers but less obvious for others.

- If you can't find a support group that suits your needs, don't get discouraged. Conduct online research or ask trusted family members and friends for their recommendations. You may even decide to start your own group. In today's connected world, your options are endless.

14
Finding Purpose

Hmmm, what is the meaning of life? That question has been pondered ever since people had free time to ponder. I am not asking you to solve this esoteric, mystical question. For your mental health, I am encouraging you to think of some goal outside of yourself that may give you pleasure to be a part of. The goal is not necessarily to make it happen (like ending world hunger), but to find satisfaction in knowing you are engaging in something helpful to others.

It's not a secret that finding purpose in your life will increase your emotional well-being, spirituality, and reason for living. While this chapter may overlap with previously mentioned topics (e.g., nutrition, exercise, hobbies, socializing), I would like you to think of Finding Purpose as a reflection of a guiding principle in your life.

Examples may involve some of the following guiding principles. In the parentheses, you'll find a leading organization in that field.

- Animal rights (World Wildlife Fund)
- Disabled children (Special Olympics)
- Building/working (Habitat for Humanity)
- Environmental/conservation (Greenpeace)
- Education/leadership (Teach for America)
- International development (Peace Corps)
- World health (Doctors Without Borders)
- Hunger (Feeding America)
- Mental health (American Foundation for Suicide Prevention)
- Equity and inclusion (National Urban League)
- Bruce's passion (Partnership Ethiopia)

EXERCISE 14: FINDING PURPOSE

If you are interested in finding a purpose, focus on one or two of the guiding principles listed above and implement some of the following steps to get started:

- Highlight one or two guiding principles on the previous page.
- Keep an open mind.
- Practice gratitude.
- Explore your passions.
- Be part of a community.
- Volunteer.
- Find inspirational people.
- Educate yourself.
- Join a cause.

Find purpose. The means will follow."
— Gandhi

15
Reframing Your Mindset

Reframing your mindset and dealing with repressed feelings are two of the guiding principles of this manual. I suggest rereading page 16 in section 1, "Reframing Your Mindset/Repressed Feelings." Here are the highlights: Based on the thousands of patients I have seen over the past 40 years, a typical person lives in the low or moderate end of the emotional spectrum about 80 percent of the time. Because of this, please focus on managing these feelings and placing them in the right frame. Learn how to handle or accept them when they arise, but focus on feelings of happiness, contentment, pleasure, bliss, joy, peace, love, fun, and silliness. It takes effort to reprogram your brain from dwelling on negative feelings to focusing on positive ones. I assure you, it can be done.

Steps to Reframing Your Mindset

Let's start with recognizing and reframing "low moments." Next time you are aware of negative emotions creeping in, do the following:

- First, sit with the feeling. Try it on. Let it do its thing. Don't fight or deny it.

- While doing this, slowly connect the emotion to the situation causing it.

- Here are some questions to consider:
    - What's bothering me?
    - Where in my body do I feel this emotion?
    - Have any stressors occurred lately?

- When you find the connection, try recognizing the specific feeling and reason. (It's OK if you can't make the connection or identify the cause.)

- Don't analyze it or judge it; recognize it.

- Take a moment to reflect on the reason for the feeling and allow yourself to understand it.

Eventually, identifying the trigger of your feelings will allow you to deal with them directly and do something about them. For example, many of my patients recognize their low mood was related to a recent encounter with a family member, friend, or co-worker. It didn't go away because they didn't allow themselves to feel, process, or respond. It took on a life more significant than it should. In hindsight, many said the situation wasn't very important or traumatic, but ignoring it (intentionally or not) made it worse than it needed to be.

Find perspective through contrast. For example: I don't feel good today, but I realize others worldwide are much worse off.

— Bruce

EXERCISE 15: REFRAMING YOUR MINDSET

If reframing your mindset appeals to you, practice the steps on page 96.

Don't give all of yourself to anyone. Don't rely on one person for your happiness.

— Bruce

16

Practicing Forgiveness

Are you mad at someone right now? Many people would answer *yes* to that question. Here's even worse news. Many who answered yes don't realize how much this anger saps their energy and happiness. Hanging on to negative feelings can be a heavy burden—so heavy that it can lead to chronic depression, anxiety, and stress.

Letting go of ill feelings can help bring peace of mind and allow you to make more room for love, kindness, and empathy. However, forgiveness can be a complicated task. Journaling and talking with a trusted companion or therapist can help begin this process.

The following excerpt is from one of my patients:

"After a year of seeing him, Bruce encouraged me to start the process of forgiving both my ex-wife and her lover for their affair. I was trying to understand why he called it a process. At first, it was impossible. But he would occasionally bring it up as a topic to deal with. Over time, I just kept trying. Every fiber of my body wanted to stay angry and hurt. But I kept practicing. Yes, it required practice, lots of practice. There were no magic pills or shortcuts. I kept practicing, the same way you practice learning an instrument, new language, or athletic skill.

"I would purge my anger about it with Bruce at our sessions, and then I would think of reasons to forgive them:

- My sons would benefit.

- God is the only one who gets to decide a punishment.

- Staying angry made my health worse.

- I wanted my children to have both parents in their life.

- We needed a highly functioning parenting team.

In hindsight, many things about our marriage upset me. Now, I see that I am happier without my ex. If I had not chosen to forgive her, I would not have realized this. There's an old saying, 'The best way to get back at the person who hurt you is to be happy.'"

One of the guiding principles of this book is to apply loving kindness to everything you do. Forgiveness is no different. Show loving kindness to your enemies, because if you don't, you can't forgive; if you can't forgive, you are trapped in anger, sadness, and disappointment.

Do not let the behavior of others destroy your inner peace."
— Dalai Lama

The weak can never forgive. Forgiveness is the attribute of the strong."
— Gandhi

EXERCISE 16: PRACTICING FORGIVENESS

Should you choose to practice forgiveness, try the following exercise:

- Make a list of one or more people you are having trouble forgiving.

- Add a reason why you are holding on to this anger. What is the benefit?

- Now, write the benefits of forgiving them.

- Undoubtedly, you discovered forgiving far outweighs holding on.

- Now, start the process of forgiving.
  Here are a few options:
    - Forgive them silently in your heart
      (if they are unavailable or unsafe to contact).
    - Write a note and send it to them.
    - Write a note and don't send it to them.
    - Donate to an organization that reflects their favorite cause.
    - If applicable, ask your higher power to forgive.
    - Say something nice about them behind their back (good gossip).
    - Tell that person you forgive him or her.

Don't expect anything from the people you are forgiving. You are not doing this to appease them or make them feel better. One of my patients shared that he forgave his father for his parenting flaws. His father was an alcoholic and emotionally abusive during his upbringing. When he forgave his father in person, the father didn't know what behaviors he was referring to. Don't forget to apply loving kindness to everything and everyone you meet.

One of the most courageous decisions you'll ever make is finally letting go of what hurts your heart and soul."
— Unknown

17
Self-Compassion

Have you ever noticed how patient, understanding, tolerant, and forgiving you are to others? Even if they did something foolish? Well, today is "National Cut Yourself Some Slack Day." If you can do it for others, why not try it yourself?

Remember to cut yourself slack when encountering inevitable bumps and bruises. Self-compassion is being understanding, encouraging, and kind to yourself, even in the face of setbacks.

Furthermore, self-compassion can enhance performance and professional growth and directly correlate with high self-esteem. When you are kind to yourself, you are more likely to succeed.

I believe self-compassion is a loftier goal than self-improvement. Self-improvement depends on many factors, many of which are out of your control. You can't rely on self-improvement to maintain your self-esteem. It can't be counted on and isn't an accurate barometer of self-value. Self-compassion, on the other hand, doesn't depend on outside factors or luck. It's a matter of treating yourself with loving kindness, care, and support as you would treat a good friend.

Moderation is important to inner peace. You don't have to do everything in excess. It's okay to be average in parts of your life.
— Bruce

EXERCISE 17: SELF-COMPASSION

- Note or, better yet, write down one or more qualities you are particularly hard on yourself about. A few examples might be your performance at school or work, how you treat others, your health or appearance, or your relationships.

- Place that list of qualities in your pocket. While it's in your pocket, try to notice when you are being hard on yourself on those topics.

- When you catch yourself being hard on yourself, replace self-criticism with self-compassion. In other words, how would you have encouraged someone who did the same thing? Remember to exude loving kindness in these situations.

- What were the words you used to encourage them?

- Let that be a mantra (a statement repeated to help influence positive self-change) you tell yourself every morning.

- Don't be afraid to edit the mantra to fit your current life.

- Focus on one behavior at a time.

- Once you have replaced self-criticism on that topic, try another.

Disclaimer: This is not meant to excuse yourself for a behavior you are indeed falling short of. For instance, arriving late for work every day. You have control over that. You don't have control over your height or occasional random mistakes.

RECIPE 5: APPLE-RAISIN BREAD PUDDING

Chef Bruce says, "If it's a little comfort food you crave, try this twist on Martha's bread pudding."

Prep Time: 30 minutes
Total Time: 90 minutes
Yield: 8 servings

Ingredients:

- 5 cups milk
- 6 large eggs
- 1 1/2 cups granulated sugar
- 1 tablespoon vanilla extract
- 1 1/2 tablespoons grated orange zest
- 2 teaspoons ground cinnamon
- 1/2 teaspoon salt
- 4 cups cinnamon raisin bread (about 1 pound), torn or cut into small pieces
- 2 red apples, peeled, cored, and thinly sliced
- 1/2 cup dried cranberries
- 1/4 cup golden raisins
- 4 tablespoons unsalted butter, melted
- 2 tablespoons cold unsalted butter, plus more as needed

Directions:

1. Preheat oven to 350°F. Butter a 9 x 13-inch baking dish.

2. In a large bowl, whisk together milk, eggs, sugar, vanilla, orange zest, cinnamon, and salt. Add in the bread.

3. Cover with plastic wrap and weigh down the floating bread with another bowl.

4. Let stand until bread is soaked through, about 20 minutes.

5. Fold in apples, cranberries, raisins, and melted butter.

6. Pour into prepared baking dish. Dot the top of the bread pudding with pieces of the cold butter. Bake until set and lightly golden on top, 50 minutes to an hour.

7. Serve warm.

Inspired by the Martha Stewart Test Kitchen.

RECIPE 6: MY BEST PUMPKIN BREAD

Chef Bruce says, "This is my favorite recipe for those fall blues. It's packed with sweet cinnamon spice, loads of pumpkin flavor, and, if you want, chocolate chips. I use more cinnamon than the original recipe calls for. Included is an optional orange glaze for those desiring even more pizzazz."

Prep Time: 15 minutes
Total Time: 75 minutes
Yield: One loaf

Ingredients:

- 1 3/4 cups all-purpose flour
- 1 teaspoon baking soda
- 2 1/2 teaspoons ground cinnamon
- 1/2 teaspoon ground nutmeg
- 1/4 teaspoon ground cloves
- 1/4 teaspoon ground ginger
- 3/4 teaspoon salt
- 2 large room-temperature eggs
- 1/2 cup granulated sugar
- 3/4 cup packed brown sugar
- 1 1/2 cups pumpkin puree

- 1/2 cup vegetable oil
- 1/4 cup orange juice
- 2/3 cup semisweet chocolate chips (optional)

Optional Orange Glaze Ingredients:

- 1 cup confectioner's sugar
- 1 orange, zested and juiced

Instructions:

1. Adjust the oven rack to a lower position and preheat the oven to 350°F.

2. Grease a metal 9 x 5-inch loaf pan.

3. In a large bowl, combine the flour, baking soda, cinnamon, nutmeg, cloves, ginger, and salt until combined.

4. In a medium bowl, whisk the eggs, granulated sugar, and brown sugar together.

5. Into the wet ingredients, whisk in the pumpkin, oil, and orange juice. Pour these wet ingredients into the dry ingredients and gently mix using a wooden spoon. There will be a few lumps. Do not overmix. Gently fold in the chocolate chips, if using.

6. Pour the batter into the prepared loaf pan. Bake for 60–65 minutes, loosely covering the bread with aluminum foil after 30 minutes to prevent the top

from burning. The bread is done when a toothpick inserted in the center comes out clean. Begin checking around the 50-minute mark.

7. Allow the bread to cool completely in the pan on a wire rack before slicing.

8. Leftover pumpkin bread can be covered and stored in the refrigerator for up to a week.

Optional Orange Glaze Directions:

Whisk confectioner's sugar, 1 tablespoon orange juice, and orange zest in a bowl. Add more juice to achieve desired thickness. Drizzle over cooled pumpkin bread.

Inspired by Michelle B. and sallysbakingaddiction.com/pumpkin-chocolate-chip-bread.

18
Setting Boundaries

Is there someone in your life who upsets you because of one of the following reasons?

- They are too nosy.
- They expect too much.
- You feel unappreciated or used.
- You feel unsafe or uncomfortable.
- They embarrass you.
- Their actions make you feel disrespected.

Setting boundaries will have a noticeable and positive impact on your emotional well-being. Learning to set clear boundaries will make you feel safer and more appreciated. Practice saying "NO!" There is more to setting a boundary than that, but it is a great start.

Right now, practice saying "no" to the following questions:

- Can I borrow $100? No.
- Can you work extra hours this weekend? No.
- May I have a kiss? No.
- Can you drive me to work? No.
- Can you lie for me just one more time? No.
- Insert your own here. Say it out loud.

For example, your neighbor asks you to pick up a few groceries on your next trip to the supermarket. This request happens often. It causes you to feel used. You decide it involves too much time and sometimes money (as she constantly needs to remember to pay you back). A simple "I won't be able to do that" will suffice. Don't make excuses or little lies because people can argue those. A simple "I won't be able to do that" is enough.

You don't have to tell everyone your underwear size.

— Bruce

EXERCISE 18: SETTING BOUNDARIES

- List the areas in which you wish you had more boundaries.

- Next, prioritize the list.

- Starting with #1, visualize how you might react next time someone moves too far into your boundary.

- Practice saying "no" with strength, but without anger.

- Practice how you will react if that person becomes confrontational.

- Remember, you don't owe anyone a lengthy explanation about your reasons for saying "no."

A 'no' uttered from deepest conviction is better and greater than a 'yes' merely uttered to please or, what is worse, to avoid trouble."

— Gandhi

Why do you think that people want what you think they need? People tend to get emotional about other people's business.

'Why don't they have children? Why don't they find a job that pays more? Why don't they lose or gain weight? Why don't they go to church more? Why do they dress like that?'

Quit judging and worrying about what other people are doing, who they are with, or what color they are. Just love them.

— Bruce

We need to judge less and understand more."

— Mitta Xinindlu

19
Asking For Help

If you are not used to or are uncomfortable asking for help, you are forgoing one of the most effective methods of improving your mental health. Readers who have discovered this know what I am talking about. However, for many, seeking the assistance of others can be daunting.

If you're feeling overwhelmed or stressed, remember to speak up and lean on those around you, such as family, friends, and colleagues. If you are uncomfortable asking for help, start by taking baby steps. If you are uncomfortable asking the person who can best help you, find someone who can help connect you.

For example, David, who had quadriplegia, wanted to educate children about how to speak, help, and interact with people with disabilities. He wasn't comfortable contacting the head of a school or an administrator in charge. He sought advice from his good friend who taught school for 20 years. His friend suggested he start by contacting the people he knew who had kids in elementary school. The rest was easy. The friends who knew David were eager to reach the correct people at their school on his behalf. He became a highly sought-after speaker in no time. Eventually, he became comfortable reaching out to the people in charge.

Don't put more of yourself into a relationship or situation than you get out. Some might wonder if this applies to volunteering, where you may not receive any pay or recognition. Think about that one a bit before answering."

— Bruce

EXERCISE 19: ASKING FOR HELP

If you would like to start asking for help, consider the following:

- Write a list of one or more areas of your life that you wish were better.

- Prioritize these challenging areas.

- Starting at the top of the list, find someone in this realm who could help you. These could be individuals you don't know or someone you know intimately.

- Without thinking too hard about what you will say, contact them via phone, text, or email, and ask for their help getting started.

While I encourage you to travel outside your comfort zone, I am not suggesting that you do something reckless or unsafe.

20
Medication

I purposely saved the discussion of pharmaceutical medication for last. In my experience, the mere mention of medicine causes stress for many.

Taking medication is a decision that your medical doctors, therapist, family, and you decide. Mostly you. It can be scary getting started. I suggest trying some of the first 19 methods discussed in this section before delving into pharmaceutical medication.

I have witnessed countless success stories about patients taking medications. They tend to be more successful when accompanied by talk therapy and one or more of the methods discussed in section 2.

Taking meds does not mean that you have or are being diagnosed with clinical depression or any other diagnosis. For people not diagnosed with depression, meds can be effective when dealing with a particularly intense event or period (e.g., grieving the loss of a loved one). However, less seemingly chaotic events can affect different people in different ways. Therefore, I encourage you *not* to compare your reaction to a particular stressor with how others appear to deal with a similar stressor.

Be aware that sometimes it takes a while for a new medication to work correctly in your system. Finding the effective medication and dosage may take some trial and error. This is common because drugs affect different people in different ways. It is not an exact science.

Brain chemistry may contribute to an individual's depression and may factor into his or her treatment. For this reason, antidepressants might be prescribed to help modify one's brain chemistry. These medications are not sedatives, "uppers," or tranquilizers. They are not habit-forming. Generally, antidepressant medications have no stimulating effect on people not experiencing depression. Antidepressants may produce some improvement within the first three to four weeks of use, yet full benefits may not be seen for two to three months.

If a patient feels little or no improvement after several weeks, a psychiatrist can alter the dose of the medication or add or substitute another antidepressant. In some situations, other psychotropic (the universal category of mental health prescription drugs) medications may be helpful. You must inform your doctor if a medication does not work or if you experience side effects. Psychiatrists usually recommend that patients continue to take medication for six or more months after the symptoms have improved. Longer-term maintenance treatment may lower the risk of future episodes for high-risk people.

EXERCISE 20: MEDICATION

If you're pondering medication for situational mental health reasons, consider the following:

- If you see a therapist recommending a medication evaluation (or want to learn more), contact your primary care physician (PCP), psychiatrist, or other trusted medical professional. Tell them how you are doing. Find out their recommendations concerning medications.

- Ask your doctor about pharmacogenetics (DNA testing that helps discern the best medication for your unique body and brain).

- Be prepared to give specific health information, such as:
    - Your history of taking pharmaceutical medications
    - Your experience with talk therapy
    - Anything occurring in your life that may be causing an increase in worry, fear, and sadness (See section 1, "Depression Is Different Than Normal Waves of Emotion" for a list of everyday stressors.)

- The results and date of your last physical checkup
- Any significant medical conditions (physical or emotional)
- Any current medication and over-the-counter medications you take

The above is not a test to determine if you need to be medicated or have depression. As previously mentioned, this manual is not focused on clinical depression. If you feel you have it, contact your psychiatrist, PCP, or other qualified medical professional. Also, refer to section 1, "Do I Have Depression?" for more information.

 *Love is the key to everything good. Just imagine everyone and everything emitting their highest level of love (joy, peace, kindness, tolerance, acceptance). What would this look, sound, smell, taste, and feel like? Don't forget to include the environment, world, and universe.*

— Bruce

Closing

My career has brought me great joy and fulfillment, especially working with patients. I hope this book will bring you joy, peace, and happiness.

My theme in life is simple: *LOVE*. I would be gratified if this book helps you love yourself and others more.

Please keep this guide handy and refer to it when needed. I know I do.

Don't hesitate to contact me with your stories, feedback, and progress. I can be reached at bas4400@aol.com. I would enjoy hearing from you. Wishing you all the best!

Love,
Bruce A. Schmidt, MA, LPC, LCPC, ABMPP

Resources

The following resources were used to research content for this book:

Cleveland Clinic. https://my.clevelandclinic.org/.

Dweck, Carol S. *Mindset: The New Psychology of Success.* New York: Ballantine Books, 2006.

Feiereisen, Sharon. Reviewed by Vivek Cherion. "How much water should you drink every day? Plus Signs You're Hydrated." June 6, 2024. *Real Simple.* https://www.realsimple.com/health/how-much-water-to-drink-day.

"Four Mental Health Tips fors Creating an Even Better 2022." Harvard Pilgrim Healthcare. https://www.harvardpilgrim.org/hapiguide/4-mental-health-tips-for-creating-an-even-better-2022/.

Hoy, Toni. "Types, Benefits, and What to Expect." Last updated on March 12, 2024. Helpguide.org. https://www.helpguide.org/articles/therapy-medication/support-groups.htm.

Mayo Clinic Staff. "Water: How much should you drink every day?" October 12, 2022. Mayo Clinic. https://www.mayoclinic.org/healthy-lifestyle/nutrition-and-healthy-eating/in-depth/water/art-20044256.

"The Nutrition Source: Water." Harvard T.H. Chan School of Public Health. https://nutritionsource.hsph.harvard.edu/water/.

Ruiz, Don Miguel. *The Four Agreements: A Practical Guide to Personal Freedom.* San Rafael, California: Amber-Allen Publishing, 2001.

Sarno, John E. *Healing Back Pain.* New York: Grand Central Publishing, 1991.

"Taking Action: Healthy Sleep Tips." Harvard Medical School, Division of Sleep Medicine. https://sleep.hms.harvard.edu/education-training/public-education/sleep-and-health-education-program/sleep-health-education-68#.

"31 Tips to Boost Your Mental Health." Mental Health America. https://www.mhanational.org/31-tips-boost-your-mental-health.

Troyer, Angela K. Reviewed by Jessica Schrader. "The Health Benefits of Socializing." June 30, 2016. *Psychology Today*. https://www.psychologytoday.com/us/blog/living-mild-cognitive-impairment/201606/the-health-benefits-socializing.

"What Is Depression?" American Psychiatric Association. https://www.psychiatry.org/patients-families/depression/what-is-depression.

Williams, Ebony. "5 types of friendships we need, according to experts." *The Atlanta Journal-Constitution* (April 25, 2023), https://www.ajc.com/life/5-types-of-friendships-we-need-according-to-experts/WCIZLQ45ABCRPBCWEYT5HQVJ6M/.

Wooll, Maggie. "Finding your North Star: Uncovering your life's purpose." BetterUp. Feb. 20,

2024. https://www.betterup.com/blog/finding-purpose.

About The Author

Bruce Schmidt has practiced psychotherapy in medical and outpatient settings for more than 40 years. He is a licensed professional counselor in Missouri and a licensed clinical professional counselor in Illinois. He is board certified as a medical psychotherapist and disability analyst.

He is the former director of adolescent treatment at Our Lady of Grace Child Center and director of integrated medicine at St. Louis Cancer and Breast Institute. Bruce is currently in private practice in St. Louis. Over the past 20 years, he has worked collaboratively with friend and psychiatrist Rebekah Radmanesh, MD.

Bruce is co-founder, along with Gayle Bogenschneider, of Partnership Ethiopia, a not-for-profit organization whose mission is to improve the lives of the people of Ethiopia through educational opportunities, accessible health care, and local business development.

 *There is only one way to happiness: to cease worrying about things beyond the power of our will."*

— Epictetus